The Future
of
Family Court

STRUCTURE, SKILLS AND LESS STRESS

Bill Eddy, LCSW, CFLS

Author of *Managing High Conflict People in Court*

PRESS

The Future
of
Family Court

Contents

"What sort of flowers say, 'I promise to obey the restraining order'?"

CHAPTER ONE

Disorders in the Court

THIS BOOK IS DESIGNED FOR family court judicial officers, although I realize it may be read by other professionals and individuals involved in family court themselves. It's
written from my perspective as a family lawyer and mental
health professional, and as a trainer of judges in managing
high-conflict people in court. I am not a judge and I do not
presume to know how to do the difficult work judges do day
in and day out. Yet I have represented clients in family courts
for 15 years and I have heard many of the concerns of judges
in my seminars and private conversations.

The emphasis of this book is to apply lessons learned from the
field of mental health to the family court system, especially
in regard to working with parents with personality disorders

or traits. Prior to my legal career, I was a therapist working with children and their parents in psychiatric hospitals and outpatient clinics. This background has given me a different perspective on today's families in family court. Yet my emphasis here is on what individual judges can do, rather than recommending sweeping changes in the court system or creating new players in the decision-making process.

From my experience and observations, the majority of families appearing in family court today with high-conflict disputes include one or both parents with a mental health problem presenting as a legal problem. Most of these mental health problems include the following characteristics:

1. The person is not aware that he or she has a mental health problem.

2. The person does not change their dysfunctional behavior, despite feedback.

3. The person "externalizes" responsibility for their problems and feels helpless.

PERSONALITY DISORDERS

These three characteristics are common for people with personality disorders, although not all people with personality disorders become "high-conflict" people (HCPs). The HCPs are the ones who blame a specific person for their problems and become preoccupied with attacking that person verbally, legally, financially and sometimes violently. They pull others into this blaming process (family, friends, children, therapists, lawyers, mediators and judges), some of whom become their Negative Advocates – people who aggressively defend and justify the HCP's behavior to others because they are "emotionally hooked," rather than informed about the situation. For an introductory explanation and four methods of managing HCPs, see my prior booklet for judges: *Managing High Conflict People in Court* (HCI Press, 2008).

Recent information on personality disorders seems to indicate that they are increasing in society as a whole, and especially with each younger age group. The United States National Institutes of Health (NIH) has completed a large study of over 35,000 people, designed to be representative of the United States population. (This study was not complete when I wrote *Managing High Conflict People in Court*.) The final results include the following regarding the five personality disorders I consider the "high conflict" personality disorders:

Prevalence of Personality Disorders
National Institutes of Health Study by Age Groups

Narcissistic   6.2% of general U.S. population

Age Groups
65+   3.2%
45-64   5.6%
30-44   7.1%
20-29   9.4%

Borderline   5.9% of general U.S. population

Age Groups
65+   2.0%
45-64   5.5%
30-44   7.0%
20-29   9.3%

Paranoid   4.4% of general U.S. population

Age Groups
65+   1.8%
45-64   3.6%

30-44	5.0%
20-29	6.8%

Antisocial   3.6% of general U.S. population

Age Groups
65+	0.6%
45-64	2.8%
30-44	4.2%
20-29	6.2%

Histrionic   1.8% of general U.S. population

Age Groups
65+	0.6%
45-64	1.2%
30-44	1.8%
20-29	3.8%

The researchers posed the theory that the higher percentages in the younger age groups and the lower percentages in the older age groups may indicate that personality disorders fade with time. However, that theory conflicts with everything I have learned about personality disorders, which is that they are maintained fairly consistently over the lifetime as are all personalities. In a correspondence with the head of the study, they acknowledge that they do not have any evidence supporting their theory. It would actually take a similar study ten years from now to see if today's young adults became less disordered as they aged. It is unlikely that another such study will occur.

A second theory is that people with personality disorders don't live as long. This may be true, because of their increased levels of high-risk behavior, substance abuse, anxiety, depression, suicide, and serious health problems. Yet this appears unlikely to explain the significant difference across the age groups.

The third theory – which I subscribe to – is that personality disorders are rapidly increasing in society, so that each younger generation is growing up with a higher percentage of personality disorders. For example, narcissism is reported as much higher since the 1970's, according to studies of college students. This may be the result of the self-esteem movement, which encouraged parents and teachers to praise children for being special – regardless of effort or learning skills. Thus, they grew up with a sense of entitlement seriously out of proportion to their achievements. The next generation appears on track to have this problem as well.

"THE MAJORITY OF FAMILIES APPEARING IN FAMILY COURT TODAY HAVE A MENTAL HEALTH PROBLEM PRESENTING AS A LEGAL PROBLEM"

Likewise, our culture has increasingly placed an emphasis on high-conflict behavior in movies, television, video games, the Internet and in the news. While such behaviors are attention-getting entertainment for adults, research suggests that they may become absorbed in personality development for some children. The cultural over-emphasis on violence and litigation as methods of resolving disputes has grown dramatically in the past two decades, so that each generation's young adults have more and more of these characteristics embedded in who they are. It may be that the characteristics of personality-disordered parents are passing to their children – and that high-conflict cases in family court are contributing to this process.

If so, we may have an opportunity to reduce the risk of more children developing personality disorders as they grow up by making important changes in family court. It appears time to take seriously the impact of personality disorders on the way we manage the adversarial process of family court.

Therefore, in this booklet, I recommend (and predict) two major paradigm shifts for family courts which do not require any changes in laws or procedures, and which judges can immediately implement on their own to make their decision-making more effective, less stressful and more appropriate for personality disorder parents (or any parents). However, these changes will ideally be done throughout a court juris-diction, so that the expectations, training and shared imple-mentation can make them even easier to apply for judicial officers, saving time and money on a system-wide basis.

These two paradigm shifts are:

- Skills before Decisions (for most cases)
- Behavior Pattern Analysis (for the more difficult cases)

SKILLS BEFORE DECISIONS

Teaching conflict resolution skills to people with mental health problems before the big decisions are made is an important – and realistic goal – for family courts. People with these problems, including personality disorders, have a narrower range of behavior than the average person, yet the way you handle them can bring out their best or worst behavior.

An important shift in how you handle them is to expect them to learn and practice simple conflict resolution skills, so that they will be able to make more of their own decisions, to cope better with your decisions, and to use these skills in the future with their children and the other parent. This empha-sis on conflict resolution skills places a stronger burden on parents to manage themselves and participate in decision-making to their maximum ability, while reducing the work-load – and stress level – of the court.

Skills

This skills approach is a shift from viewing parents with mental health problems as one-dimensional people, who are incompetent as parents, who can be evaluated as though frozen in time, and who can never change. It is true that these are tendencies of these parents, because of their narrower range of behavior. However, I have learned from my experience working with clients in psychiatric hospitals, in outpatient clinics and in my family law practice, that most people with mental health problems have abilities that can be built upon to resolve most of their disputes – if there is sufficient structure and if they are required to learn and use the proper relationship conflict resolution skills.

Relationship conflict skills are different from pure adversarial skills, which have no concern for the future existence of a relationship between the parties. Relationship conflict resolution skills must operate in the moderate emotional and behavioral range, so that they don't destroy the underlying relationship. These skills cannot be learned in a primarily adversarial environment and they cannot be learned without being reinforced by everyone around the person. Also, these skills are best taught and practiced in a relationship, so that a generic parenting class or online course may be less effective or insufficient for many of those with personality disorders – although parenting classes or online courses can still be helpful in addition to the skills training I describe.

Structure

This book is designed to provide alternatives for "structuring" parents that can be used immediately in your courtroom, as well as proposals that I hope will be applied to court systems over the next decade.

Less Stress

The emphasis on skills for parents will shift the emotional burden from the court to them. Not only will this reduce judicial stress, but it will actually reduce the parents' stress, as they become more active and successful participants in the decision-making process to their maximum ability (rather than feeling like helpless recipients of justice or injustice), while teaching their children positive coping skills at the same time. My experience shows that parents with mental health problems appreciate learning conflict resolution skills and find that they can apply them in other areas of their lives.

Long term potential

Therefore, I believe the future of family court should provide a structure for parents to learn and use conflict resolution skills – before the big decisions are made. Simply giving them a decision (no matter how well-reasoned) does little to change their lives and often makes things worse, as they negatively prepare for court and negatively respond to the outcome of court decisions. Often the court's decision is like a speed-bump in their drive to dominate and control what others do. For example, many of the worst custody battles occur after the divorce has been finalized. Some divorces in family court last longer than the marriage! (See example in Chapter Two)

"MOST PEOPLE WITH MENTAL HEALTH PROBLEMS CAN RESOLVE THEIR DISPUTES - IF THERE IS SUFFICIENT STRUCTURE AND THEY ARE REQUIRED TO LEARN AND USE THE PROPER SKILLS."

A structure that focuses on relationship conflict resolution skills gives parents the opportunity to make their own decisions to their maximum ability, to accept court decisions when the court has to make them, and to resolve conflicts with the other parent and their children as they go forward in their new lives. This point is emphasized throughout this booklet in my suggestions for any courtroom today and proposals for system-wide implementation in the future.

PATTERN ANALYSIS

For those who are unable to resolve their disputes by learning relationship conflict skills, the court will need to make their decisions for them. However, in today's family court, much of the decision-making, especially regarding parenting, is done by focusing on one or two seemingly extreme behaviors or events – without the context of the person's pattern of behavior. Based on these isolated behaviors or events, long-term parenting decisions are made which may or may not be in the child's best interest. Family court judges – especially new judges – are often making a best guess, based on the demeanor of the parties and the strength of arguments.

Unfortunately, in family matters the emotions surrounding these events, and the dramatic arguments made by the parties and/or their counsel, tend to make it harder to discern the truth, rather than easier. The adversarial process may work well with normal people in litigation, but it does not work well with family court litigants with mental health problems that are being exaggerated or minimized for a legal advantage.

People with personality disorders, in particular, can be very convincing and misleading in their courtroom presentation of self. Yet they have recognizable and predictable patterns of behavior that become obvious when these patterns are examined.

Some of the most responsible parties can be made to appear incompetent in court by someone with a personality disorder or their Negative Advocate, as many responsible people do not try to hide or shape their frustration, confusion and doubts. This is particularly true of antisocial domestic violence perpetrators, who can appear very charming and reasonable in court, and their victims, who can be made to look very incompetent and emotionally unappealing in court.

> "PEOPLE WITH PERSONALITY DISORDERS CAN BE VERY CONVINCING AND MISLEADING IN THEIR COURTROOM PRESENTATION OF SELF. YET THEY HAVE RECOGNIZABLE AND PREDICTABLE PATTERNS OF BEHAVIOR THAT BECOME OBVIOUS WHEN THESE PATTERNS ARE EXAMINED."

Credibility and Cognitive Distortions

Determining credibility is usually one of the biggest issues in any legal dispute in court. For example, cross examination is considered the engine of the truth. However, when someone with a personality disorder is involved, there are two major problems with credibility:

1. A personality-disordered person usually believes in their many cognitive distortions (see *Managing High Conflict People in Court* for more about cognitive distortions). In these cases, trying to assess whether such a person is lying or telling the truth totally misses the issue of whether the underlying information is actually true or false. Such a person may be totally honest – and totally wrong.

2. A personality-disordered person often projects onto the other party bad behavior that is more like their own. The passion with which such a person attacks and criticizes the other party can seem compelling. ("The other party must have done something terrible to have upset this person so much.") Yet this sincerity may come completely from their cognitive distortions as well. Such a person may seem very credible and sympathetic – and totally wrong.

These two problems of people with personality disorders confound family courts more and more. Most of their litigated cases involve disputes over the basic facts, so that judges are tempted to decide the case based primarily on the appearance of credibility.

Presenting the Pattern

Therefore, a new approach to this problem is to have the parties present a pattern analysis of their own behavior and of the other party's behavior. This includes showing how often negative behaviors have occurred (just once or on numerous occasions) and showing what positive behavior patterns are as well. This assists the court in more truly understanding what is going on for each party, and avoids the preoccupation with one or two dramatic events – which may or may not represent the past pattern of behavior.

The importance of using such an approach will be discussed

near the end of this book, along with a brief demonstration of one method of pattern analysis. By seeing patterns over time, we can more accurately assess levels of risk with each party and times of risk. This information can be much more helpful than debating one or two events or statements, in determining future parenting behavior and potential risks of harm to the children or the other party.

The Importance of Less Stress

A recent study of the ten most important parenting skills taken from decades of research determined that two of the top three are not even specifically about parenting:

1. Love and affection for your child.

2. Ability to manage your own stress.

3. Demonstrating healthy relationship skills with other adults.

While managing one's own stress as a parent is the number two skill, parents involved with family court hearings are extremely stressed – both in preparation for the hearing and after the hearing. It is common for attorneys to report that their clients don't remember what happened in the court-room, they are so stressed and confused.

Children

The stress of the parents transfers directly to the children, even when they try to protect their children from knowledge of an upcoming court hearing. However, high-conflict parents freely share court information with their children and sometimes eagerly bring them to court to testify against the other parent. From my experience with about 40 alienation cases, much of a child's rejection of one parent occurs after the court process begins. The child absorbs the parent's stress emotionally, and often develops a disproportionately strong dislike for the other without really knowing why. This alienation happens to some mothers and some fathers, but always when there is a parent with a personality disorder involved, from my experience and observations.

Non-personality-disordered parents are usually able to protect their children from their battles, although they can't avoid sharing their visible stress. Having one's parents in a contest over them is highly distressing. The most frequent feedback I hear from counselors is that the children just want their parents to stop fighting. They don't care about the schedule as much as ending the conflict.

From my experience as a lawyer in family court and as an out-of-court mediator, one of the biggest differences in court cases is that the parents are unable to communicate without tension (if at all) after they have completed a court battle over a parenting issue.

One wonders whether parents should be allowed to fight over parenting plans in court at all, when the end result is an inability to co-parent thereafter. Few legal professionals realize how big an impact the decision-making process has on the long-term relationship of parents with mental health problems.

Judges

Of course, the impact on judges is significant as well. Many judicial officers tell me how frustrating and stressful it is to make rulings and orders for angry and upset parents, who provide limited or unreliable information, who often won't follow the orders, and possibly will behave worse after court decisions are made. They say they are frustrated when they have to decide between two "fit" parents, or between two lousy parents. Less often do they have a clear-cut case of one great parent and one lousy parent. It's common knowledge that the majority of judges in family court seem glad to move onto civil and even criminal court calendars after their term is up in family court.

Family Lawyers

The stress on family lawyers has driven many of the best to abandon family court litigation for mediation, collaborative divorce, and other forms of out-of-court settlement of cases. Many family law attorneys will not take parenting litigation cases, although they still appear in court on financial and other matters. There has been a universal shift worldwide in family courts to have more and more parties representing themselves. Many judicial officers report that they believe a majority of self-representing parties have mental health problems.

Mental Health Professionals

For the past thirty years there has been an influx of mental health professionals into the family court process, as coaches and counselors for parents involved in parenting conflicts, and increasingly as custody mediators and psychological evaluators – who often play the strongest role in the decision-making. Judges like to rely on the opinion of mental health professionals, who usually have far more training in the issues at hand.

But now, many mental health professionals are informing me that they are trying to reduce their court caseloads. Some therapists will no longer take cases if there is an active custody and access dispute. Some evaluators are avoiding court cases, after the past decade with a record number of lawsuits and administrative complaints against them by clients, who cannot sue the judge but can bring board complaints against evaluators.

The Public

Even the public gets involved, as high-conflict people bring their complaints against mental health professionals, judges and attorneys to the news media – some of whom become unwisely and emotionally hooked into the drama, while others are wisely able to avoid these controversies, which never get clearly resolved.

The public also gets involved as taxpayers, because of the rapidly expanding use of family courts over the past decade for resolving parenting matters. With a single hearing costing approximately $600-$800, and numerous hearings for each judge each day, the cost of family court conflict is financial as well as emotional. Many sources report that high-conflict family court cases are increasing, and there is no end in sight.

Murder-Suicide

Lastly, some individuals with serious mental health problems simply cannot handle the stress of family court. We see in the news an increasing number of murder-suicides related to divorce – many involving children who are killed as well. It is hard to determine if these are being reported more or if they are truly increasing. What is clear is that many of them occur within a week or two of a family court hearing – either before or after – and some occur on the same day as the hearing.

Thus, the importance of finding solutions that reduce the

stress of family court on parents, judicial officers, lawyers, mental health professionals – and especially the children – is critical. It is my belief that making the paradigm shifts I discuss in this book will assist in reducing this stress. While many states and provinces are reviewing and changing their court procedures (allowing children to testify, adding parenting classes, creating new professional roles, etc.), I do not believe that court procedures alone will make much difference.

Family courts need to make a paradigm shift from being the decision-maker regarding parenting schedules for "fit" parents (which includes the majority of high-conflict parents), to providing structure and skills so that these parents can make their own decisions to their maximum ability. Then, judicial officers can focus more on making truly legal decisions and safety decisions, when dangerous behavior is accurately identified warranting legal restraints.

While the focus of this book is on parenting disputes, mental health problems drive most of the financial hearings in family courts today as well. Therefore, the same principles can be applied to all family court matters: more structure, more skills and less stress.

CHAPTER TWO

Setting Limits

A JUDGE IN CANADA decided that both parents had "overused" the family court system, so he barred them both from having any further hearings without court permission. The Globe and Mail reporter, Paul Waldie (2008), quoted the judge as saying:

> *"The parties have gorged on court resources as if the legal system were their private banquet table. It must not happen again… Both sides have shown an inability to abide by court orders such that their access to this court should be restricted… Some day, a wise person in a position of authority will realize that a court of law is not the best forum for deciding custody and access disputes, where principles of common sense masquerade as principles of law."*

The reporter further described the case:

> The couple [was] married for one year and have an eight-
> year-old daughter. Under their divorce, the mother won
> custody and the father received extensive access. Their
> legal battle has centred mainly on terms of the access
> and it has dragged on for seven years, involving 12 dif-
> ferent judges, a dozen lawyers, 25 court orders, 2,000
> pages of court filings, three contempt motions and one
> suspended sentence.

At one point the mother, 32, was so paranoid about the father she
pulled the girl out of a good school just because the father attended
a meet-the-teacher day, according to court records. She also took
the child to dozens of medical appointments in the hope of finding
a doctor who would support her allegations of emotional abuse by
her ex-spouse, court records show.

Last year, Judge Quinn convicted the mother of contempt for vio-
lating a court order at least 19 times. He said she showed "not a
hint of remorse, only a re-doubled intention to prove her conduct
correct."

The judge said the father, 38, withheld child support and failed
to make contributions to an education fund for the child, but still
spent more than $200,000 fighting the case with a 'scorched-earth'
mentality. The father was so "hot-headed, stubborn and suspi-
cious" that when Judge Quinn was considering punishment for
the mother's contempt, the father pushed for a 30-day sentence.

> "Had the father taken a more noble and forgiving
> approach, had he, for example, asked the court not to
> send the mother of his daughter to jail, I believe that
> his request would have shrunk the rift between both
> sides from a chasm to a crack, making possible a tol-
> erable peace," said the judge, who issued a suspended
> sentence. "That day, all chance was squandered for the

child ever to comfortably breathe the name of one of her parents in the presence of the other...." (A12)

The Judge's Dilemma

Most family court judges are familiar with the above types of high-conflict cases and they are frustrated by them. For the past seven years I have provided seminars and training to judges on dealing with HCPs. They are eager for tips about how to handle the above emotional issues with respect and efficiency, while doing their official job of making legal decisions. They have huge case loads, an often thankless job and diminishing resources. Yet I have never met a group of more sincere and wise people, who care deeply about children and families.

This presents a dilemma to judges: How do you efficiently resolve issues for people with deeper problems, when "the issue's not the issue?" Up to now, many judges have used anger, shame, lectures, threats, setting strict limits, and so forth. On the other hand, many use patient listening, friendly comments, humor and words of encouragement. Most judges I have observed use some combination of both.

Some judges crack down hard on the apparently offending party:

For example, one judge felt helpless to reconcile a 15-year-old daughter with her father, so he focused his anger on the mother:

> "She is alienating the child against her father. She is behind this decision and if there was any way I could punish her for it, I would. But I have no legal authority to do so, so I am just going to leave her with my message – that I believe she is ruining

her child's life."

Other judges try to appear balanced in their frustration, like the judge who said: "All I see before me are two pig-headed parents who don't care about their sons."

Unfortunately, none of this is effective in dealing with a "high-conflict person" (an "HCP"). In fact, such statements usually escalate the HCP parent. In the "ruining her child's life" comment, the mother was already extremely anxious. By criticizing her publicly, her anxiety increased, which increased her fear and anger toward the father, which of course spilled over emotionally to her daughter, which may have strengthened her daughter's resolve to avoid the conflict – by avoiding her father.

In the "pig-headed parents" case, the father had a history of domestic violence against the mother and an intense drive to control their sons. The mother was a quiet woman who was very careful to do everything the court told her to do, including not discussing the case with her sons and not expressing frustration about the father in their presence. So when they were both criticized at court, it escalated the father – who became more demanding and controlling – and discouraged her. From her point of view, the judge had joined her abusive husband in criticizing her, once again.

Both approaches of reprimanding a parent can add to alienation. There is a high likelihood that the emotional absorption and reaction to them will be passed on to the children by one or both parents, which will make their children more anxious, and more likely to "split" their parents into all-good and all-bad to resolve the conflict.

The judge in the opening example above was right. What are custody and access (visitation) disputes doing in court anyway? Court is an adversarial process and by its structure it promotes a Culture of Blame which is contagious and increases family stress. While lawyers, judges and most ordinary citizens in the past were able to cope with this adversarial process, today's increasing population of high-conflict people cannot handle it. They lack the ability to contain their upset emotions and to restrain their extreme impulses during the process of litigation.

High Conflict Cases are Different

Many judges agree that there needs to be a different role for the court in high conflict cases. In arguing for more case management with high conflict cases, the Honorable Justice Donna J. Martinson (2010) has stated:

> While professionals may not agree on the exact nature of alienation or on what the best responses should be, it is crystal clear that in alienation and other high conflict cases the stakes for children are high. They can be seriously damaged. The longer the problem continues, the more harmful the situation can become and the more difficult it will be to resolve. Not only is harm caused by the alienating behavior and the conflict associated with it, but the court process itself may exacerbate the conflict, placing the children in the middle and affecting their lives on a daily basis in highly destructive ways. There are also long-term adverse consequences for children including but not limited to difficulty forming and maintaining healthy relationships, depression, suicide, substance abuse, antisocial behavior, enmeshment, and low self-esteem. (180-189)
>
> ….

In alienation and other high conflict cases, it is exceedingly difficult to achieve the goal of a just, timely and affordable decision on the merits. These cases involve a disproportionate number of people with personality disorders (which can involve lack of insight into the parent's own behavior, blaming the other parent, seeing oneself as victim, and a disregard for authority and the law), mental health issues, substance abuse problems, and patterns of controlling behavior. These traits manifest themselves in the court process, in a number of concerning ways, at the instance of one or both parents, and at all three stages of the process [pre-resolution stage, resolution stage (trial) and enforcement stage]. (181-182)

....

"As a result, one or both of the parents is financially and emotionally drained. Not infrequently the more disturbed parent exhausts or frightens the other parent into a settlement that fails to meet the needs of the children. The children may be irreparably harmed by the litigation process or settlement. (182)

....

Alienation cases are almost always high conflict matrimonial cases. We need a system where we can stream out the high conflict cases and deal with them immediately. (185)

[Quoting Phil Epstein and Lene Madsen]

....

Case management by the same judge can be critically important in dealing with high conflict cases. Mental illness or personality disorders are commonly a component of high conflict cases. The illness or disorder is often not immediately apparent. Familiarity with the 'problem' litigant promotes an understanding (sometimes even a more sympathetic understanding!) of that litigant. (187)

[Quoting Justice David Aston of Ontario Superior Court of Justice.]

One Judge Per Case

To effectively help families help themselves, it helps to have one judge throughout the case who can truly manage the case and set limits on inappropriate behavior. When I started practicing law in 1993, one of my earliest cases involved allegations of child sexual abuse. Over the course of the case, we had nine hearings with seven different judges before it was resolved. A few years later, our court system went to an "independent calendar" system, in which a case was permanently assigned to one judge who ran his or her own calendar. It is hard now to imagine what it must be like without such a system.

Forget About Insight

People with personality disorders or traits often look like ordinary people who just are stressed about the divorce. They may appear logical and reasonable and able to manage themselves – except for one or two "indiscretions." What isn't obvious, is that they truly think differently and very defensively. Every aspect of the court process is a potential issue: cooperating with procedures, cooperating with court orders, accepting loss and moving on, responding to settlement proposals, and so forth. It is the ordinary-appearing nature of personality disorders that makes them so confusing and in need of a different approach. They do not self-manage very well.

> "THE KEY TO MANAGING HIGH CONFLICT PARENTS IS TO REALIZE THAT THEY DON'T NEED MORE SELF-EXPRESSION; THEY NEED MORE SELF-RESTRAINT."

People with personality disorders or traits need a much tighter family court, which can supervise and set limits on their litigation behavior and extreme parenting behavior. High-conflict parents are truly different in regard to their lack of self-awareness, preoccupation with blame and lack of behavior change. They cannot be expected to self-manage their own high-conflict behavior, based on insights you try to give them through lectures, persuasion, anger or compassion. Forget about insight, since they lack self-awareness (hard as it is to believe). They need structure, skills, consequences and encouragement. The rest of this book describes some methods of providing for these needs that actually reduce the amount of work, time and stress you need to spend on these cases.

The key to managing high-conflict parents is to realize that they don't need more self-expression; they need more self-restraint. They repeatedly defeat themselves – with their partners and their children and the law – through their excessive drive for self-expression. By setting limits on their high-conflict behavior, we do them a favor. But professionals must provide the structure so that they can learn and practice skills of self-restraint.

CHAPTER THREE

Structure and Accountability

A MAJOR THEME IN THIS BOOK is that high-conflict parents often raise high-conflict children, who learn to become abused, abusive and/or alienated in their present and future close relationships. The way to avoid this tragic outcome is to have the children learn and practice three basic skills for resilience (flexible thinking, managed emotions and moderate behaviors), rather than learning or reinforcing the skills of "splitting" they so often learn from their parents. (Splitting is the mental health concept in which a disturbed person sees some people as all-good and others as all-bad, with no gray areas). Family courts can help parents, children and society by focusing more on these three skills and less on making parenting decisions for parents.

The role of the family court must be to provide more structure – placing more responsibility on parents for reasonable settlement (while protecting them from abuse) – and requiring more accountability. It's much like raising a teenager. This requires a shift in how judges think about and relate to high-conflict parents, rather than any substantive change in laws or procedures – although some may be necessary in some jurisdictions.

It is important for judicial officers to restrain themselves from the urge to make all of the decisions for high-conflict families, in an effort to reduce the conflict. Without involving the parents in learning skills and increasing their ability to make some decisions, however minor they may be, making decisions for them will not reduce the conflict and will be a waste of time. Instead, judicial officers should take charge of such families by taking charge of the structure and accountability – not making most of their decisions.

Structure for Learning Skills

How should high-conflict cases be handled differently by the judge? It's important to recognize that their problem is a lack of the three conflict-reducing skills (flexible thinking, managed emotions, and moderate behaviors). For whatever reason, high-conflict parents cannot stop themselves from self-harm and from harming their children. One or both parents is truly "out of control" – they can't control their all-or-nothing thinking, their unmanaged emotions and their extreme behavior. Abuse and alienation are two symptoms of their high-conflict personalities. More than having decisions made for them, they need to be required to learn and use these basic skills. The courts actually have the opportunity to help them get started, while still supervising them.

First, courts need to provide a structure for high-conflict parents. Right from the start of a potentially high-conflict case, judges should order parenting classes or short-term counseling that teaches them to work on these three basic conflict-reducing skills.

How does the judge know that it is a potentially high-conflict case? When one or both parents seek to restrict the other's parenting time. (That is when the author's New Ways for Families method is designed to be ordered, as described in a later chapter of this book.) Such restrictive requests almost always trigger a "parent contest" which rapidly escalates both parents' defensiveness – which is passed on to the child.

Courts don't need to wait for an evaluation of abuse or alienation to know that high-conflict behavior may be just around the corner. When the parent contest begins is when alienation will begin to grow, as HCP parents engage in more and more splitting to "win" the parent contest – whether the HCP parent is the initiator of the court's involvement or defending against allegations, or both – and the child begins to absorb one or both parent's high anxiety, stress and anger.

A request for restricted parenting means something is seriously wrong in the family. This should trigger three theories of the case in the judge's mind:

1. the "restricted" parent is an HCP and needs restrictions because of out-of-control behavior, such as domestic violence, child abuse or substance abuse;

2. the parent requesting restrictions is an HCP with a personality disorder or traits and is distorting the other parent's reasonable behavior; or

3. both parents may be HCPs with serious problems. In all of these cases, putting both parents into a parenting class

or short-term counseling at the start of the case will benefit both of them and their children, and help head off a high-conflict case. We already know what skills they need.

Of course, the court should concurrently make temporary orders, such as temporary protective orders, temporary child support and temporary parenting plan. By making orders for boosting their conflict reducing skills, the court shifts the focus onto both parents to work on themselves, rather than just focusing on the accused. This helps avoid splitting, lowers HCP expectations of vindication or revenge, and sends the message that court is really not where they belong with their parenting issues.

Second, courts need to follow up with accountability at all future hearings. When the parents return to court, the judge should first quiz them on what they have learned in their parenting class or counseling, before considering any motions before the court. HCP parents won't use these skills, except by repetition and being constantly reminded by professionals. The court should make clear that it is their responsibility to be solving their parenting problems reasonably, and will only make decisions for them after all other reasonable methods have been exhausted. The court should be a very reluctant decision-maker in the area of parenting for high-conflict parents.

CHAPTER FOUR

The Trouble with Making Decisions

MOST JUDGES LIKE MAKING DECISIONS and are very good at it. However, with high-conflict people, the issue's not the issue! As the case in Chapter 2 demonstrates, with HCPs the issue is their personality-based lack of conflict resolution skills and insecure relationships. They bring one issue after another to court for the judge to decide. Ironically, the better you are at making decisions for them, the more likely they are to depend on you for more in the future.

Yet the court never satisfies them – and cannot satisfy them. What they are really looking for is:

- Vindication – that he or she is the "good parent" and that the other parent is the "bad parent," for everyone to see, once and for all. Court is where vindication is officially bestowed in our society. (Particularly characteristic of Borderline HCPs.)

- Respect – to make up for all the disrespect the person has received in his or her life. Court is where one can prove that he or she is a superior person and that the other parent is grossly inferior in every way. Being granted custody is the ultimate award. (Particularly characteristic of Narcissistic HCPs.)

- Revenge – for abandoning the relationship, which may have been the most secure relationship the person ever had. Humiliation in the public process of Court is the most powerful weapon in today's society that is accessible to anyone. (Characteristic of Borderline, Narcissistic, and Antisocial HCPs.)

- Protection from internal fears – to help insecure people feel safe from their frequent and extreme fears. Court has the power to lock people up, keep them away, and teach them a lesson so they will stay away forever. In today's frightening world, the courts will protect you. (Characteristic of Paranoid HCPs.)

- Dominance – to put the other person in their place and dominate them again. Court is where one can regain control of someone who is beginning to act too independent. He or she can draw the person back into their life by serving papers requiring attendance at hearings, by serving subpoenas, by taking depositions, by delivering documents requiring responses, by demanding hundreds of personal documents, by seeing each other at court for hearing after hearing. (Characteristic of Antisocial and Borderline HCPs.)

- Attention – to finally be able to tell one's story to the person with all the power. To have one's "day in court." Court is where one is allowed to freely use all of the drama one can muster, including tears, anger, charm, vulnerability, witnesses and evidence on one's behalf to exclusively focus on blaming an "all bad" person. (Particularly characteristic of Histrionic HCPs, but all of the above.)

It is for these reasons that you don't want to create a dependency on you for making their decisions. You cannot get it right, because you are missing the point. The decisions they want are based on feelings – such as feeling vindicated, protected, dominating of the other party. Since legal decisions cannot meet such personality-based feelings, they will never be satisfied in court.

Strongly Promoting Settlement

Hopefully by now it is clear why I am promoting settlement efforts in cases of HCP parents – who lack settlement skills. This is a huge opportunity for family courts to help children by requiring their parents to learn conflict resolution skills and to practice them in their parenting and at court. This may only be at a very minimal level, but this must become an expectation of the court. When judges and other professionals make brilliant decisions for parents, it removes the motivation for them to learn to make any decisions themselves for their family. Therefore, judges should repeatedly quiz parents on what they have learned and how they have practiced their skills.

The more that judges send the message that settlement is the standard expectation, the more that parents will try to fulfill that expectation. Praising them for their successes means a lot to HCP parents, who are constantly looking for validation from the court. It's better to give validation for small successes in reaching agreement with the other parent, than for big "wins" against the other parent.

Treatments for personality disorders have been showing us that many HCP parents may be able to change, with sufficient structure, learning small skills in small steps, and enough encouragement. Therefore, courts should shift the burden to parents to acquire and practice their skills in making decisions about their children. Judges should resist the urge to just make the decision for them, as much as possible.

I remember one day when I was in court and heard the judge addressing an attorney, his client and a self-representing party. The judge told them to go into the hallway and try to settle their issue of the day.

10-15 minutes later, they came back into the courtroom without an agreement. The judge said that it was unlikely he would have time to address their matter after all that morning. They would have to come back in the afternoon. However, he suggested that they try one more time to settle their issue by negotiating in the hallway. It was obvious that the lawyer was really upset about this, as he apparently needed to be in another court that afternoon.

A few minutes later, they returned to the courtroom. When the judge had a moment during another lengthy hearing, the attorney announced to the judge that they had reached an agreement. The judge immediately stopped his present hearing and invited the lawyer and the parties to come forward and recite their agreement for the court record – to make it a binding agreement and court order.

The message of the morning in that courtroom was that serious negotiations will be expected of everyone, and that settlements will always take precedence over arguments in the judge's schedule. It was an ideal example of shifting the burden to the parties to resolve their dispute.

Resist the Urge to Fix It

Judges are great at making decisions. They are wise, well-educated, sincere, and like solving problems. Therefore, it's hard to get them to hold back and put the burden back on the parents to make decisions to the best of their ability. However, it is far better for the parents to struggle with using their flexible thinking in making proposals, to struggle with learning to use managed emotions, and to reflect openly on their extreme behaviors.

They may not be perfect and may make less sophisticated decisions than a judge. However, it will be better for peace in the family and better for the long-term impact on the children. Their parents should struggle with these responsibilities and develop their skills, rather than running to court to get a brilliant decision from the judge each time a problem arises.

When the judge decides – or a court mediator or other professional – HCP parents interpret it to their children something like this:

Mom: "Well, the judge decided that your father cannot pick you up Friday until 6pm. The judge is concerned about how much time you have with him."

Dad: "The judge is keeping me from picking you up at school. He doesn't understand how unfair that is, so I am meeting with my lawyer to try to change that. Hopefully, pretty soon I can pick you up at your school."

However, if the parents have to resolve that issue:

Mom: "Well, your father and I agreed today that he can pick you up at 5pm at my house. It's not what I prefer, but it's what we agreed."

Dad: "Your mother and I agreed that I will pick you up at 5pm. She didn't want me to pick you up until 6pm, but we reached an agreement. So make sure you're ready to just come out of the house. I don't want us to argue around you."

This is a small step. With time, each parent may become more able to drop the additional comments after their first sentence above. This may seem like such a minor issue, but high-conflict parents have difficulty making any agreements. Yet most of them can make decisions if professionals restrain themselves from doing it for them and require them to learn and practice skills for making decisions. If one parent is not an HCP, that parent can be a role model of making proposals and focusing on the future, not the past, in making decisions. It's important not to assume both are HCP parents.

Of course, decisions regarding protection may need to be made by the court. But as many decisions as possible should be made by the parents – much more than occurs today with high-conflict families. The "fight or flight" response of many courts and other professionals is to get angry and make the decisions for them. We have to resist that urge, so that the parents can practice skills that will benefit their children.

Mediation and Collaborative Divorce

The court should expect parents to make these decisions outside of the courtroom, either through mediation, collaborative divorce, attorneys assisting them in negotiating, or other means. This obviously takes more work on the part of the parents, but these methods have more lasting rates of success and don't escalate the whole family into more dysfunction before and after decisions.

If necessary, a Parenting Coordinator (described below) may be helpful. The point is that the greater participation of the parents in their own decisions, the better it is all around. We shouldn't allow them to give up so easily and just make the decisions for them. The cost is too high, for all the reasons described in this little book.

Of course, once the decisions are made, the court may require that the parents cannot keep changing them, so that one HCP parent is not constantly manipulating the other. The place to start is to require them to learn the skills and practice them in small steps – then hold them accountable.

Domestic Violence and Abuse

In cases of domestic violence or child abuse, the same skills of flexible thinking, managed emotions and moderate behaviors apply. By requiring the parents to practice these conflict-reducing skills, you may help them reduce abusive behavior as well. We know that most perpetrators of domestic violence or child abuse are going to have a future relationship with their children, so it will help to give them some tools to make it better, beyond simply stopping hitting.

High-conflict cases usually include allegations of child abuse, domestic violence, substance abuse, false allegations and/or child alienation. While judicial officers are encouraged to order skills training, they will still need to address the allegations. It is important to acknowledge that a parent "might be right" when he or she says that the child has been abused. There must be no presumption that there isn't abuse. It must be investigated somehow.

On the other hand, there should be no presumption that there is abuse. It's important for parents to know that their concerns are taken seriously, but that many aspects of children's behavior are not automatic signs of abuse or intentional alienation, such as statements or behavior.

Having the parents learn and practice these three skills of flexible thinking, managed emotions and moderate behaviors, will help the court in making its future decisions. When the parents come back to court, the judge should ask them what they have learned from their class or counseling. Their answers should help the judge see who is trying to change and who is not. Then, the judge should ask them how they would deal with a hypothetical parenting problem in the future. This will help the court see how they are applying their skills – or not. The court can always wait and see if the parents are able to make improvements, then order assessments for those who appear unable to do so.

In short, shifting more of the burden to the parents to learn and use conflict resolution skills will help the parents become more responsible, help protect their children from unresolved conflicts, and help the court in making more useful decisions.

CHAPTER FIVE

Eliminating the Parent Contest

A BIG STEP IN MANAGING high-conflict cases is to eliminate the parent contest, in which each parent attacks the other and defends himself or herself, and gets stuck in all-or-nothing thinking. If there are parenting behavior concerns, then they should be addressed as problems to solve, rather than competitions to win. The point is to avoid making it a contest between the parents – to avoid the dangers of splitting and the children absorbing a battle, which will affect their future relationships.

Instead, the court should expect each parent to compete with himself or herself. If a parent has engaged in abusive behavior, then the court can say:

"While you are working on your issues, the other parent is going to have most of the parenting time. But this will be temporary, if you can demonstrate improvement to the court. For now, the other parent will fill in for your parenting time. This is not a contest with the other parent. It's an expectation by the court that you will succeed and that I will be able to have you spend your parenting time with your child yourself in the future. I hope that is the case at our next hearing."

Such an approach eliminates the contest and any sense of victory for one parent. Instead, it is more like a helping hand while one parent works on himself or herself. It's important to give high-conflict people hope. (Of course, highly agitated, angry or paranoid parties would not be appropriate for this statement, as they will be too resentful of the other parent's "victory" in any form to see the benefit to themselves.)

With such an approach, the court and professionals can keep the focus on future behavior, while ordering the appropriate treatment. "Yes, there was an abusive incident. Now, let's see if you can learn to manage your own emotions better so that your behavior never reaches that point again."

Ironically, many HCP parents don't want the other parent to change and improve their behavior and their relationship with the children. They just want to eliminate the other parent – a splitting approach. This may become obvious as courts and professionals emphasize learning skills over making extreme decisions.

3 Key Questions

The court can reinforce this accountability at any time by asking each parent to tell the judge:

- Three positive traits or skills of the other parent (to avoid all-or-nothing thinking)

- Three ways that the parent is protecting their children from their upset emotions during the divorce (to avoid contagious unmanaged emotions)

- Three behaviors they are using to avoid conflict with the other parent (so they are consciously avoiding extreme behaviors, rather than being impulsive)

Such questions of the parents provide a proactive way of preventing bad behavior, rather than trying to correct it afterwards. Most HCP parents want to succeed, but have a hard time controlling themselves. These questions substantially shift the focus to future behavior, rather than past disputed behavior. This may reduce defensiveness, which is a barrier to positive behavior change, and should help protect the children from the conflict.

If you are going to ask the parents the above questions, it helps for them to know about it in advance and to think about it and prepare their answers. This preparation reinforces the importance of being accountable in this fashion.

One possibility is to give all parents a notice that these three questions will be asked at their first court hearing. If the parents know these questions are coming, it will put their other requests into perspective and their answers may help the court know a little about their thinking. The more reasonable their answers, the less likely they are to be high-conflict parents. Of course, this should not be the only factor to consider, as some HCPs can be very smooth and convincing at the start.

Equal Empathy, Attention and Respect

Parents and professionals are used to court being a place for shame and blame. Lawyers shame and blame parents, and judges shame and blame parents (and sometimes lawyers). HCPs need the reverse. They are much more responsive to validation and empathy.

At one court hearing, the court denied my client's motion for a reduction in child support. Then the judge said: "I can understand that it must feel like you are the only one hitched up to the plow and pulling." When we left the courtroom, I asked how he felt about that decision (with which I disagreed). He didn't like the decision, but he said: "The judge understands what it feels like to be in my shoes. I don't need to fight his decision." And that was the end of it. Over the years, we settled whatever issues arose and never went back to court.

High-conflict parents are looking for empathy, attention and respect from the court and legal professionals, because they aren't getting these from the people around them – because of their own self-defeating behavior. The average person just seeks legal decisions and usually can settle their case once they know the law. HCPs want more, and they don't even realize this.

This empathy, attention and respect must be provided very equally. HCP parents are very sensitive to being compared and losing. Since their issues are really personality-based, the importance of being interpersonally equal must not be lost in decision-making. The most effective judicial officers I have seen remain calm and are very equal in their eye contact, tone of voice, and comments to each parent, even while making decisions that strongly favor one side or the other.

For example:

> Ma'am, you might be right that the father has been abusive with the children and that is why I am giving you this temporary protective order. Sir, you might be right that the mother is misrepresenting events or that they are totally not true. I will need more information at the next hearing to help me understand what is really going on.

> However, you should both know that when you ask me, a stranger, to make your decisions for you, one or both of you may be disappointed. Therefore, I encourage you to reach your own agreements as much as possible. I am also going to order you to participate in a short conflict resolution skills program before our next hearing. I am ordering you both to take this without any assumptions about either one of you, as you both will need to use these skills in the future regardless of what has happened in the past.

> You will benefit in learning new ways to deal with the other parent. If the other parent is a difficult person, that is all the more reason to learn and practice these skills. Your children will benefit from both of you taking this program.

CHAPTER SIX

Managing High-Conflict Emotions

REGARDLESS OF THE ISSUES, judges can immediately impose the following seven steps at hearings, to reduce the emotional intensity and risk of adding stress to the parents, and indirectly to their children.

1. That all presentations must include positive information about the other parent, if negative information is going to be presented. (To avoid all-or-nothing thinking.)

2. That all presentations must include more than one proposal or solution to the problem. (To focus on the future and avoid all-or-nothing thinking.)

3. That each parent must explain their efforts to solve the problem before using the court process. (To avoid reinforcing

using the court to solve parenting problems.)

4. Inform the parties that statements should not emotionally compare one parent to the other as a better person. (To
   reduce splitting.)

5. That no physical gestures, such as finger-pointing, raised
   voices, puffed up anger, and dramatic accusations will be allowed. (To avoid emotional contagion.)

6. All presentations must be matter-of-fact, with information
   presented in as neutral terms as possible when describing
   concerning behavior, including abuse. (To avoid emotional
   contagion.)

7. Before the court hears evidence about the other parent's
   negative behavior, the court should require that each parent must describe examples of their own parenting behavior
   problems and efforts to change. Or each parent should be
   quizzed on hypothetical parenting examples in which they
   can describe how they will use flexible thinking, managed
   emotions, and moderate behaviors.

All of this structure puts the burden on the parents to focus
on improving their own behavior, as well as focusing on the
other party. HCP parents seek to avoid responsibility and
place it on the court's shoulders – then complain or appeal
when the judge doesn't "get it right."

It is unfortunate that such civil behavior must be spelled
out, but we are all learning that high-conflict parents – and
some high-conflict professionals – lack the ability to stop
themselves. Therefore, it will take the court and reasonable
professionals to stop them from their destructive behavior. It
will take more than a reprimand or angry feedback from the
bench.

Remember that HCPs lack self-awareness and lack behavior

change. Trying to "make them see" the inappropriateness of their own behavior will fail – they will vigorously defend it as normal. Instead, they need much more structure for how they speak in court and much more intervention from the court when they misbehave. We have learned, the hard way, that HCPs need lots of structure – to keep them out of trouble. Matter-of-factly stopping inappropriate behavior and routinely requiring positive behavior, like that described above, may be more constructive.

HCPs also respond better to positive feedback and encouragement, than to criticism and efforts to shame them into good behavior. In a sense, the court holds the power to provide elements of a "secure relationship," by being consistent, being predictable, not over-reacting to their upset emotions, focusing them on the next task and encouraging them on their way.

Emotions Right Before or After a Hearing

HCPs have a predictable pattern of extreme behavior when they anticipate or experience loss, whether real or just perceived. These perceived losses include:

- Loss of "attachment" to their partner or their child
- Loss of high self-esteem
- Loss of control over the other person or whole situation.

Court hearings are when many of these "losses" occur. Therefore, right before or after a hearing – often within the week and sometimes the same day – they engage in their worst behavior. Here is the pattern:

1. The party has a personality disorder, combined with a history of extreme behavior.

2. There is a moment of perceived serious loss, such as at a court hearing.

3. There is an impulsive over-reaction to the loss with extreme behavior.

Times of High Risk Related to Court Hearings

- A party serves papers on the high-conflict person (HCP) that request court orders the HCP feels as a severe threat of loss (such as regular contact with a child).

- The HCP prepares for the court hearing and becomes obsessed with the potential loss.

- At the hearing, the court makes orders against the HCP; or the HCP wins and feels empowered to punish the other party for the hearing with extreme behavior.

- The HCP loses more time with the child than he/she expected.

- The legal case ends, so regular contact with the other party will end.

Examples of Extreme Behaviors in Response to Losses

- Domestic violence

- Child abuse

- Kidnapping the child

- Alienating the child

- Making false allegations

- Spreading rumors

- Verbally attacking the other party publicly, the other attorney, the judge

- Filing lawsuits, board complaints, appeals against professionals involved

- Suicide attempts; actual suicides

- Murder of spouse, children, and/or self

What Can Be Done About this Pattern?

I believe that parties and professionals need to be educated about this pattern and be prepared for extreme behavior before and after a hearing that could represent a serious perception of loss. (Remember, it's how the HCP perceives it – not whether you consider it a serious loss. For example, loss of an hour of parenting time may be devastating to an HCP, but not recognized by professionals as significant.)

In the most extreme cases, there should be a cooling off period of a week or two when a possible HCP loses a hearing, such as visitation at a visitation center or at the court, where there are metal detectors, for the period right before and after a potentially disturbing hearing with a high-risk personality.

Significantly Different Emotional Behavior

Legal professionals tend to treat high-conflict people as ordinary people going through a hard time. I want to repeat that we need to realize that they are not ordinary in how they handle their emotions and how they handle losses – especially relationship losses. We need to plan ahead for these predictable times of extreme emotions and extreme behavior, so that we can help the parties restrain themselves at the key times of risk. Simply telling them to behave or making punitive orders will not motivate them to use skills of self-restraint they do not possess.

CHAPTER SEVEN

Children's Testimony

THERE IS A DANGEROUS TREND in some family court systems (for example, California's new rules) to involve the children more in court hearings. While the intent is designed to be inclusive for children – to give them a "voice" – the more involved they are in the adversarial process the worse the family will become. We must remember that we are dealing with disturbed individuals and their out-of-balance families.

One of the basic principles of family systems dynamics is that everyone in the family adapts to a dysfunctional person – usually by over-compensating in one direction or another. Children are especially vulnerable, because they are dependent on their parents for their survival. Children in dysfunctional families are no more free to think and express independent opinions than hostages are free to discuss their care while still in captivity. After 30 years of working with children and families, I consider creating court procedures to include children in divorce hearings as equivalent to creating procedures to make nuclear war user-friendly.

This is not to say that children's voices should not be heard. But not in an adversarial process. Ideally, counselors would assist them in sharing their concerns with their own parents. That is who should really be hearing their voices – and who should be making the parenting schedule decisions.

If that is not a healthy option (child abuse, etc.), then having a child speak with a confidential counselor will help the child more than placing a child in a quasi-decision-making role. We have added enough other people to the decision-making process (psychologists, custody evaluators, mediators, parenting coordinators, etc.) without solving the problem of high-conflict families. Turning to the children to testify as the next solution will do more harm than good.

Can Children Be Accurate Reporters?

Children can be accurate reporters of some events that happen to them. But, as a therapist, I also know that children can be powerfully influenced by their parents to make inaccurate statements, especially in families with abuse or alienation. Children say what helps them survive. In dysfunctional families, what helps children survive is more extreme behavior of their own.

A tragic case occurred when a child's statements should not have been believed. The child was Charlenni Ferreira in the Philadelphia area. She died in 2009, after allegedly receiving numerous blows to her head by her father or stepmother. Apparently she had numerous severe injuries and broken bones over several years that were not discovered until she died.

A school nurse lodged a child abuse report in 2006 and she was seen several times by various professionals. She walked with a limp, but Charlenni convinced them that she was treated by her parents "like a princess." Her child abuse case was closed in 2007. She continued to regularly attend school without further intervention until her death.

In divorce cases, many courts seriously consider the child's expressed wishes regarding where they live. In general, courts do not want to have children participate directly in the decision-making or court process. Yet when a child insists he or she does not want to live with a parent, it bears investigation. This is usually done by mental health professionals or lawyers for the children, but recent changes may increase the amount of questioning by judicial officers - such as in California, where new laws appear to encourage this. Here is an example of such a judicial inquiry:

> Q: Tell me what you think about if you stayed at your dad's more than at your mom's to, kind of, even out that you used to stay with your mom more?

> A: Well, I think that my mom might get mad instead of my dad because then my mom would never – I would get to see him more, and I won't get to see my mom – I mean, I will get to see my mom less, and I really want to see my mom more than I want to see my dad.

> Q: Okay. Have you told anybody that before? Did you tell Dr. Wilson that you wanted to see your mom more than you wanted to see your dad?

A: No, sir.

Q: Okay. When did you decide that?

A: I decided it when I was talking to the counselor, but I never did tell him that.

Q: Okay. All right. Now, if I said that your mom wouldn't get mad if you spent more time at your dad's, how would you feel about it?

A: I think that would be kind of okay.

Q: Okay. So I don't want to – I don't want to tell you what to say. But what I'm trying to find out is: Your concern about living with your dad is you wouldn't be happy or you're afraid your mom would be less happy?

A: My mom would be less happy.

So her driving concern was how her mother would feel, not what she herself wanted. This is extremely common in high-conflict cases, where the child is looking for peace at any price – even the sacrifice of the other parent. In this case, the judge made the unusual decision to give custody of the totally alienated older daughter to the mother and custody of the partially alienated daughter (interviewed above) to the father.

> As a general rule, this court disapproves of custody determinations in which siblings are separated. If the trial court identifies a compelling reason for the separation, however, then such a decision may be justified.
>
> In the present case, the trial court's finding that the present alienation between the father and the older daughter was irremediable at this time was well supported by the record. There was also evidence to support the trial court's finding that the

mother had attempted to negatively influence the younger daughter's relationship with the father. It is clear from the record that the parents are incapable of cooperating in a joint-custody situation. The trial court's finding and the record demonstrate that the trial court believed that the positive good that would result from a change of custody of the younger daughter would offset any disruptive effect that might be caused by the change in custody. The trial court had a compelling reason for separating the daughters because of the older daughter's current inability to get along with the father and the mother's negative influence on the younger daughter in regard to the father.

M.W.W. v. B.W. (2004) Ct of Civ App of Alabama, 900 So. 2d 1230, 1235-1236.

Likewise, children's behavior is not always an accurate indicator of abuse or alienation. There should be no presumptions. For example, if a child runs away from a parent to the other parent, it may be a sign of abuse but it may be a sign of alienation. I have personally seen that type of behavior more often in alienation cases than in abuse cases.

THE VIEWS OF THE CHILD

In 1989, the United Nations Convention on the Rights of the Child declared the importance of hearing and considering children's views in decisions that affect them. Canada ratified these terms in 1991, although the United States has never done so. Often called the "voice of the child," there is nothing that requires judicial officers to be the ones who hear a child's point of view. However, over the past decade there has been an increasing interest in having children's input expressed in discussion of parenting plans in the divorce process. I agree that children should have some way to participate in the process, but I strongly disagree that professionals should put children in any type of decision-making role. For all the reasons explained above, the parents should be in that role instead – if necessary, with professional assistance.

For example, the research by Jennifer McIntosh in Australia shows that Child-Inclusive Mediation is more successful than Child-Focused Mediation in high-conflict parenting disputes. The difference is that the Child-Inclusive approach has a professional meet with the children and then meet with the parents to share the children's concerns about the divorce. Then the parents use that information in making longer-lasting and more satisfying decisions.

> "DETERMINING WHO IS THE 'BETTER PARENT' ISN'T THE SOLUTION; IN FACT, IT HAS BECOME A SIGNIFICANT PART OF THE PROBLEM."

It may be tempting to have the judge meet with the children, as a short cut. However, this reduces the expectation that parents must work hard at making the good decisions and considering their children's concerns. Giving the children direct access to the judge, while the parents do not have comparable access, turns the potential power structure of the family upside down.

It must be further understood that children in high-conflict families are like prisoners in a war zone. They will say and do whatever they think is necessary to survive. Some children will say everything is fine, when it really isn't, such as Charlenni Ferreira above. And other will say everything is awful with a parent who they feel secure with, in order to placate a parent with whom they feel insecure, such as the younger sister above. If professionals don't realize this, they will make matters much worse, rather than better. The best approach is to help the parents hear their children's concerns, then to help them work on ways to make reasonable decisions based on those concerns. The judge should make those decisions only as a very last resort. A few experienced judicial officers who I have spoken with in Canada say that they dislike interviewing the children and do it less, based on their experience, rather than more. They believe it can make things worse in a high-conflict family.

Reducing Stress on Children

Scientists have learned that prolonged stress can trigger the release of excessive cortisol in the brain and body. This can cause damage to children's brain development over time, especially the corpus callosum which helps their right and left brains work smoothly together to manage problem-solving, even while being upset. We also know that prolonged stress often occurs in high-conflict divorce cases, especially those that spend a lot of time in family court litigation. In other words, prolonged conflict between a child's parents may be as serious as child abuse.

Martin Teicher (2002), the brain researcher, suggests that this can have long-term effects on the future of our culture, as follows:

> Society reaps what it sows in the way it nurtures its children. Stress sculpts the brain to exhibit various antisocial, though adaptive, behaviors. Whether it comes in the form of physical, emotional or sexual trauma or through exposure to warfare, famine or pestilence, stress can set off a ripple of hormonal

changes that permanently wire a child's brain to cope with a malevolent world. Through this chain of events, violence and abuse pass from generation to generation as well as from one society to the next. Our stark conclusion is that we see the need to do much more to ensure that child abuse does not happen in the first place, because once these key brain alternations occur, there may be no going back. (75)

Unfortunately, we live in a society that is increasingly focused on blaming individuals for complex social problems. The adversarial court process of deciding who to blame for a child's behavior is harmful – not only because it's often inaccurate, but because it pits parents against each other, which harms the children in the long run. Determining who is the "better parent" isn't the solution; in fact, it has become a significant part of the problem.

CHAPTER EIGHT

Parenting Coordinators

ONE OF THE ULTIMATE SOLUTIONS to removing high-conflict families from the Family Court adversarial process is to mostly remove the case from family court after the big decisions are made. Since high-conflict parents often return to court many times after the divorce is over, Parenting Coordinators are a valuable alternative for parents who still cannot make their own decisions. By ordering or encouraging the parents to stipulate to a Parenting Coordinator, they will have someone they can go to with petty complaints without incurring the cost of court and without the court having to deal with such petty matters.

Parenting Coordinators are usually trained mental health professionals or lawyers who have some degree of authority to resolve minor disputes between the parents. They can hear the parents on short notice and make decisions with little expense. Depending on the jurisdiction, Parenting Coordinators' decisions are enforceable or are considered recommendations which the parents can challenge at court if they feel strongly enough about the decision.

Parenting Coordinators can also recommend or order further counseling, parenting classes and/or skills-building programs, to help them strengthen their own conflict resolution skills and parenting skills. Remember, with high-conflict parents, "the issue's not the issue." If they are primarily seeking validation, revenge, dominance, and so forth, they should do it outside of court as much as possible.

However, for all the reasons I have described in this book, Parenting Coordinators (PCs) must be careful not to take on a decision-making role simply in place of a judge. Instead, they too must require the parents to learn and practice skills for decision-making to the maximum ability themselves. For example, if they have required parents to learn the skills described in the next chapter about New Ways for Families, they can then require parents to re-write their hostile emails into B.I.F.F. responses (brief, informative, friendly and firm). They can require parents to make two proposals each, whenever they bring a new dispute to the PC to be resolved, instead of making only one proposal and fighting endlessly for it. They should assist parents in helping themselves manage their emotions and using moderate behaviors in their problem-solving efforts.

If a parent threatens to go back to court to fight over the parenting plan again, the PC can use Pattern Analysis (explained in Chapter 10) to show the parents what could be presented to the court if there is a future court battle. There are cases where this alone has stopped a parent from re-litigating issues, because that parent could easily see how their own behavior patterns would appear to the judge.

Information about Parenting Coordinators can be found at the website of the Association of Family and Conciliation Courts at www.afccnet.org.

Ideally, someday, parenting schedule decisions will be made entirely out of court. The only parenting issue to be decided in the courts will be safety issues – or criminal behavior which should be decided in criminal courts. The remainder of the issues in family courts should be about property, support and related issues. Most of those decisions don't require seven years of hearings for a one-year marriage, like the case in Chapter 2.

Parenting Coordinators alone won't stop such problems. But Parenting Coordinators generally have more mental health, child development and communications training than a judge and can work in a less adversarial setting to assist the parents in using their skills to their maximum ability in solving parenting problems.

CHAPTER NINE

New Ways for Families™

NEW WAYS FOR FAMILIES is a new method developed by High Conflict Institute, which integrates many of the principles described in this book. It is an interdisciplinary method that teaches and reinforces relationship conflict resolution skills for potentially high-conflict parents.

New Ways for Families emphasizes short-term counseling to reduce the impact of conflict on the children in potentially high-conflict cases. It can be used whenever a parent or the court believes one parent needs restricted parenting (supervised, no contact, limited time), at the start of a case or any time a parent requests restricted parenting – including post-judgment litigation.

This method emphasizes strengthening skills for positive future behavior (new ways), rather than focusing on past negative behavior – while still acknowledging it. It is designed to save courts time, to save parents money, and to protect children as their families reorganize in new ways after a separation or divorce, for married or never-married parents. This method can be used in family court, mediation, collaborative divorce, or even post-divorce with the assistance of a Parenting Coordinator.

Goals of New Ways for Families™

1. To immunize families against becoming high-conflict families during the separation and the divorce process.

2. To help parents teach their children resilience in this time of huge and rapid change in the foundation of their family life

3. To strengthen both parents' abilities to make parenting decisions, while relying less on experts and the courts to make their decisions for them.

4. To assist professionals and the courts in assessing both parents' potential to learn new, positive ways of problem-solving and organizing their family after a separation or divorce.

5. To give parents a chance to change poor parenting behaviors (including abuse and alienation) before long-term decisions are made. This method emphasizes learning new skills for positive future behavior.

How It Works

Step 1: Getting Started

Parents can agree to use New Ways, or a judge can order it while also making temporary parenting orders, support orders, and restraining orders. First, each parent selects his or her own Individual Parent Counselor from a list of counselors trained in the New Ways method. Then, each parent prepares a Behavioral Declaration and a Reply Behavioral Declaration, which are the only declarations provided to the counselors, along with any related parenting orders, two business days before the counseling begins.

Step 2: Individual Parent Counseling

Each parent attends 6 weekly sessions with a separate, confidential counselor, using a Parent Workbook. Both parents participate in this counseling concurrently with their own counselor, with no presumptions about who is more difficult. The focus of these sessions is strengthening and practicing three conflict-reducing skills: flexible thinking, managed emotions, and moderate behaviors.

Step 3: Parent-Child Counseling

This step includes three sessions with each parent and their child/ren, alternating weeks over six weeks. The parents share the same non-confidential counselor. They each continue using their own Parent Workbook for these sessions. The Parent-Child Counselor does not write a report, but can be called to testify at court. The focus of these sessions is having the parents teach their children the same three skills they learned in their Individual Counseling, hearing the children's concerns, and discussing the new ways their family will operate with the child/ren.

Step 4: Family (or Court) Decision-making

Finally, parents use their new ways skills to develop a lasting parenting plan with the assistance of their attorneys (if any),

Family Court Services, a private mediator or a collaborative team. If they are unable to settle the case at this point, then they go to Family Court to report what they have learned. The judge will quiz each parent on how they would handle future parenting scenarios, based on their Behavioral Declarations. Then the judge will hear the case, which may include testimony from the Parent-Child Counselor. The judge then orders long-term parenting, support, and other orders, which could include long-term restraining orders, batterers treatment, drug treatment, parenting class, a psychological evaluation, Minor's Counsel, and/or a Parenting Coordinator.

Useful in Vague Cases of Emergency

One of the common problems today for judges occurs at an initial hearing with allegations of abuse or danger of abusive behavior and requests for protective orders. Judges must make the decision of possibly exposing the child to physical harm or possibly initiating the end of the child's relationship with the alleged abuser. With very little information, courts swing both ways on this. Some judges grant all requests of restraining orders, just to be "safe." Other judges deny many requests, especially when the requesting parent is not particularly persuasive. Unfortunately, there have been some high-profile cases where the wrong decision was made.

One solution is for the judge to order New Ways for Families or some other program that involves both parents getting short-term counseling – immediately. This way, each parent has a helpful, trained professional for assistance at a crucial time (perhaps the most high-risk time) and also the trained professional has obligations to report concerns of abusive behavior if they are observed. This gives the family structure while waiting for a more thorough, informed hearing several weeks later.

New Ways for Families is designed to include the option of having the Parent-Child Counselor testify in court about his or her observations of both parents as soon as six or eight weeks into a case. Since the counselor does not serve as an expert, there is no evaluation or recommendation. This reduces the likelihood of escalating the case as much. The counselor can indicate to the court if there is an apparent need for further evaluation – or not. At the same time, this counselor can be assisting the parents in working with their children. (Of course, either parent could block this counselor from testifying by refusing to sign a release of the counselor's confidentiality. However, this in itself would be revealing to the court for making future decisions and possibly ordering further psychological assessments.)

At the time of publication of this book, New Ways for Families is being used in five court jurisdictions in the United States and Canada. Two programs in Canada have three-year grants of $500,000 to implement and study this method. Several more communities have received some training in New Ways for Families. Results of the research should start becoming available in 2013.

In reality, it's easy to start ordering cases to use the New Ways for Families method. All you need are three therapists trained in the method (a 2-day training): one for the mother; one for the father; and one as the Parent-Child Counselor. Then they use the New Ways for Families workbooks to structure the counseling. If the court plays the role of follow-up, by quizzing the parents on what they have learned and on a new hypothetical parenting situation, then the parents may apply these skills to new problem situations. At the least, this method appears to slow down parents who are preoccupied with blaming their former partners, and many of them stop returning to court.

Starting a New Ways for Families Program

There are two levels that New Ways for Families can be implemented by any court system.

A. As a short-term counseling method:

Short-term counseling is the ideal way that New Ways for Families is implemented with potentially high-conflict parents. They need a strong individual counseling relationship within which to learn, resist, learn and then practice the three key skills: flexible thinking, managed emotions and moderate behaviors. If they could easily be taught these skills in a class or online course alone, they probably wouldn't be high-conflict parents. Working with experienced counselors is essential because it is about relationship conflict skills which can only be learned in a healthy relationship.

2-day training for New Ways Counselors: In order to effectively use this new method, counselors need one day understanding the theory of New Ways for Families and how it is a paradigm shift from prior methods of managing potentially high-conflict parents. The second day is mostly a day of practice exercises, in which the counselors practice working with clients in each of the four steps described above. An important aspect is shifting responsibility to the client to really learn and practice and demonstrate the three conflict-reducing skills whenever decisions need to be made.

3-hour training for Judges and Lawyers (although

the 2-day training is best): The New Ways method only works if all professionals involved reinforce the three conflict-reducing skills during every decision-making contact. Judicial officers need to learn how to make the order for New Ways for Families with a structured motivational speech and – if the parents are unsuccessful at resolving their disputes after their New Ways individual and parent-child counseling – how to quiz the parents upon their return to court about what they have learned and how they would handle a new hypothetical parent conflict scenario. Lawyers need to assist their clients in preparing behavior declarations, motivating them to use the method, reinforcing the skills during every decision-making contact, and assisting the parents in settlement of their issues using their skills.

This method does not require much in terms of court procedures, so long as the court has authority to order counseling for parents in potentially high-conflict situations. New Ways is a counseling method and uses established cognitive-behavioral techniques in particular. However, counselors need to be specifically trained in the New Ways method to deal with the resistance of high-conflict parents and to coordinate with other family law professionals in applying it.

High Conflict Institute provides the training for New Ways for Families and provides an inexpensive Licensing Agreement to use its forms, Parent Workbooks and Professional Guidebooks.

B.   As a 3-hour class:

While less ideal than the full New Ways for Families method, High Conflict Institute also provides a 3-hour class for teaching the three conflict-reducing skills of flexible thinking, managed emotions and moderate behaviors with classroom materials, exercises and teacher instruction. These skills can then be reinforced by all professionals when decisions need to be made. This 3-hour conflict-reducing skills class can be inserted into existing programs or stand on its own.

High Conflict Institute provides the training for the New Ways for Families classroom method and provides an inexpensive Licensing Agreement to use its materials. Counselors and other instructors who teach this method should have the 2-Day Training for New Ways Counselors described above.

For more information about New Ways for Families, see www.NewWays4Families.com or call 619-221-9108.

CHAPTER TEN

Pattern Analysis

PATTERN ANALYSIS IS A NEW CONCEPT for family law professionals. It is based on the understanding that people with personality disorders and other mental health problems have a narrow and rigid pattern of behavior, which is generally identifiable and predictable. By documenting and organizing behavioral incidents, it is possible to see the big picture – the pattern – and therefore be able to assess the likelihood of future positive and negative behavior. In family court this can be especially helpful in terms of predicting parenting and levels of safety.

Why Analyze Patterns?

High-conflict people (HCPs) regularly overreact to situations with all-or-nothing thinking, unmanaged emotions, and extreme behaviors (domestic violence, making false allegations, spreading rumors, abusing children, alienating children, hiding children, hiding money, and so forth). A reasonable parent facing a possible HCP in a separation or divorce may be very worried about what the HCP will do: Will he or she lie and manipulate professionals and the court? Will the HCP take extreme and abusive action toward the reasonable parent as the separation and divorce proceed? Will the child be abused by the HCP or become alienated against the reasonable parent? These are realistic concerns which can be addressed by analyzing the HCP's pattern of behavior.

Professionals (lawyers, counselors, evaluators, parenting coordinators and others) may be concerned that other professionals will not really understand the seriousness of one of the parent's dysfunctional behavior. In high conflict cases, many professionals become focused on one or two events and exaggerate or minimize their significance. Pattern Analysis provides an opportunity to show the big picture, so that other professionals understand the case.

Parents and professionals in family court often miss the pattern of HCP behavior, which is so important in making realistic decisions and obtaining effective court orders. Fully presenting the patterns of behavior in a case to family law professionals and the court helps reasonable parents and protects children, by seeing the big picture and seeing individual behavioral events.

For example, the image on the next page illustrates HCI Pattern Analysis, developed by High Conflict Institute, to show the big picture of one parent's behavior over 16 months. Each tag can be opened to see specific documents, personal and legal, which explain each incident. Legal investigations, court hearings and outcomes can be easily shown in the context of the big picture, as well as each individual event.

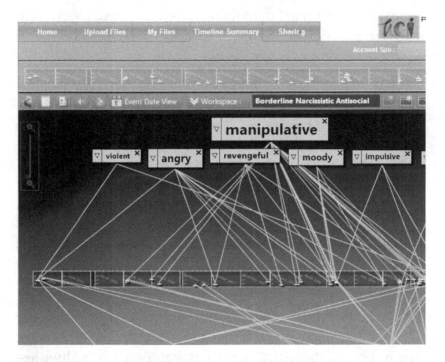

With this method, the parties and the court do not need to get caught up in emotional arguments about each event. Instead, it becomes more of a scientific analysis of the overall pattern of the person's behavior. It is hard for someone to argue that he or she would never do a specific behavior again, when there is sufficient evidence showing it has occurred six or eight times before.

On the other hand, someone who has been falsely accused of a specific behavior can show that they have never done that behavior before – that it is entirely out of character. One incident is always in the context of the overall behavior. It is a method of easily seeing the forest as well as the trees.

A court can ask both parties to provide their pattern analysis of their own and each other's behavior. Then, the details can each be examined, with authentication and testimony, if necessary, to determine if it really occurred as stated. Eventually, the court gets a clear picture of true and false statements and a pattern becomes clearly visible.

Of course, there will be antisocial litigants who try to present the other party as fitting a pattern that does not truly fit, because each tag and alleged incident is not credible. The court can ask to see what the screen looks like when you take out any particular incident. Many vague cases become much clearer once the pattern is substantiated – or not. This method can demonstrate abusive patterns and patterns of false allegations. Since HCPs frequently overreact to events, it is possible to see what types of preceding events are associated with each aggressive or otherwise inappropriate behavior. It also helps clients see times of high risk with the other party.

This approach takes much of the guess work out of basing decisions on isolated incidents. It also takes a lot of the emotion out of the process, as each party must analytically present their evidence and the pattern of their evidence. It can also be used to demonstrate positive patterns of behavior, such as the frequency of each parent's participation in school meetings, child activities and doctor's visits.

Overall, this is a method of organizing evidence, rather than replacing evidence. HCI Pattern Analysis can handle 2,000 documents in this format, which is far superior to a lawyer or party struggling to organize, find and present 2000 documents in a short hearing or even in a trial. This also avoids the issue of one party labeling the other party with a personality disorder. Instead, the pattern of actual behavior in this particular case becomes the focus of attention, rather than a label. The message is often that this pattern of dysfunctional behavior keeps repeating itself, so that strong court orders are necessary to stop it.

How does HCI Pattern Analysis™ Work?

HCI Pattern Analysis is a software service that organizes and presents numerous documents, statements, emails, text messages, police reports, hospital records, bank records, and other materials in an easy to grasp fashion for any viewer, but especially for legal professionals and the courts. With this program, a party can present a "digital timeline" showing patterns of positive and negative behavior. Many incidents can be seen all at once on the timeline, or one incident can be opened up, with one or more related documents readily available for viewing.

For example, a pattern of several incidents of abusive behavior can be shown, including dates, preceding events, severity of abuse, who was present and other information in a simple and clear manner. This avoids having one incident discounted or exaggerated, by seeing the larger pattern of repeated behavior. This also saves time struggling to find documents while a judge impatiently waits for them to be found in a stack of papers.

With HCI Pattern Analysis, you can also present patterns of false allegations, easily showing when they occurred and why they probably occurred then, such as just before pending court dates, nearing completion of a parenting evaluation, power struggles over holidays, and other precipitating events that often go with abusive behavior and/or false statements.

Parties can present patterns of missed time with the children, or preventing contact by the other parent with the children. All of these patterns are very easy to see with the graphic timeline of the HCI Pattern Analysis, rather than shuffling through piles of papers trying to find the important documents to answer the questions that the court will often want to ask off the cuff.

Who Developed this Program?

In 2010, I formed a collaboration with EVDense, a software company, to develop this software for family court cases. The method is based on my book *SPLITTING: Protecting Yourself While Divorcing Someone with Borderline or Narcissistic Personality Disorder* (New Harbinger Press, 2011, co-authored with Randi Kreger), which identifies the common patterns of these two personality disorders and how they appear in family court cases. In this book, I explain how these two personalities seem to drive many of today's high-conflict divorces, although not all borderlines and narcissists are HCPs.

EVDense had provided document organization and presentation for lawyers in many areas of law for the past ten years. We developed HCI Pattern Analysis to show patterns of behavior that are not often seen by those who only have brief contact with a high conflict person – such as family law professionals. These personalities can be highly manipulative and charming, yet they can cover up their harmful patterns very well, if you don't know what to look for and are not aware of the full pattern.

The goal, of course, is for the pattern analysis to be so accurate and easy to comprehend, that parents will agree to settle out of court after seeing the patterns of their own behavior. Parenting Coordinators have even shown their clients how their behavior looks in the pattern analysis, and had clients decide not to return to court. As of the time of publication of this book, 14 cases had used HCI Pattern Analysis, with satisfactory results for clients in all cases – some with reasonable settlements out of court and others obtaining needed court orders.

CHAPTER ELEVEN

Training

FAMILY COURT JUDGES are rarely trained in mental health problems, yet that appears to be the driving issue in the majority of cases in family court today. Many of these problems are fairly easy to understand, once you know their patterns of behavior. However, it is not necessary for judicial officers to be trained in diagnosis and treatment of personality disorders or other problems. The same general principles apply to most of these problems in family court.

As I have explained throughout this book, it is fully appropriate to require parents to focus on learning and applying simple conflict resolution skills to their parenting decisions. This does not require intensive psychological evaluations in most high conflict cases. We already know what the parties problems are: all-or-nothing thinking, unmanaged emotions and extreme behaviors.

Yet, training is essential to helping judges make the paradigm shifts described in this book. Rather than needing to acquire a deep knowledge of mental health problems, it is more important for judicial officers to learn how to structure their courtrooms and how to manage their own ways of communicating with parties who may have mental health issues. Tone of voice, tasks and consequences are the primary issues for those dealing with all of these parents.

> "RATHER THAN NEEDING TO ACQUIRE A DEEP KNOWLEDGE OF MENTAL HEALTH PROBLEMS, IT'S MORE IMPORTANT FOR JUDICIAL OFFICERS TO LEARN HOW TO STRUCTURE THEIR COURTROOMS AND HOW TO MANAGE THEIR OWN WAYS OF COMMUNICATING WITH PARTIES WHO MAY HAVE MENTAL HEALTH ISSUES."

If handled properly, and supported by all of the professionals involved, it is quite possible to help these parents learn skills to make their own decisions. Yet one of the most important aspects of this "structure and skills" approach is that judges must order parents into learning. Personality-disordered parents, because of the nature of their disorders, do not seek assistance in learning how to help themselves. They must be required to do so.

Likewise, if they are unable to reach reasonable settlements of their disputes out of court, then when they return to court they must be required to show what they have learned and how they would deal with a future conflict scenario. By making this shift to requiring greater participation in decision-making, the court reduces its own stress while helping parents become more responsible and feel more success in helping themselves.

With these principles in mind, a good training program for judges could include:

1. Learning about the five most common "high-conflict" personality disorders and related "co-occurring" mental disorders:

   Borderline
   Narcissistic
   Antisocial
   Paranoid
   Histrionic

2. Making court orders for parents to learn relationship conflict resolution skills, such as the New Ways for Families method. Such training would include:

   A. Determining when such orders are appropriate

   B. Providing motivating comments that show empathy, attention and respect

   C. Providing motivating comments that address some of the positive and negative consequences of learning and practicing relationship conflict resolution skills.

3. Quizzing the parents at the beginning of hearings, each time they return to court:

   1. What skills have you learned from your New Ways Counseling?

   2. How would you handle a situation such as the following now? (like a prior situation in which they had a problem)

   3. Assessing the potential to change, if they return to court:

After hearing what the parties have learned, after quizzing them on their responses to hypothetical scenarios (similar to those described in their court papers), the court will have a better idea of which parent(s) has the demonstrated ability to reflect on their own behavior and to make changes. The court might wish to consider the following basic categories each parent fits into regarding behavior and behavior change (observations by the Parent-Child Counselor may be necessary to assist with this):

Category 1: Generally appropriate parenting skills, with no significant problems.

Category 2: Problems in parenting, but able to make significant changes.

Category 3: Problems in parenting, and unable to make significant changes.

Category 4: Unable to determine, so additional assessment may be necessary.

The result of the above determination will help the court in making decisions regarding future treatment, if any, and future parenting restrictions, if any. For example, based on each of the above categories:

Category 1: Court would order no further treatment and no restrictions on parenting.

Category 2: Court would order further treatment and further restricted parenting, but with a review hearing in 1, 3, 6 or 12 months, whichever is appropriate for the case.

Category 3: Court would order no further treatment and order long-term restricted parenting, perhaps with a Parenting Coordinator.

Category 4: The court would order a custody/psychological

evaluation and/or the appointment of a lawyer for the child/ren (Guardian ad litem or Minor's Counsel) to represent the child/ren's interests in further court hearings.

At this hearing or a subsequent hearing, based on the evidence before the court, the court could also order drug treatment, batterer's treatment, more counseling, and/or parenting classes. A future review hearing could be ordered.

Once these orders are made, the court could order the appointment of a Parenting Coordinator to handle future disputes between the parties over the implementation of their parenting schedule. The Parenting Coordinator would need to be trained in reinforcing the use of each parent's New Ways skills when each new problem situation arises, including having them re-write emails, making proposals and practicing managing their own distress.

Such training could occur in 6 hours or ideally in 12 hours (2 days). Since working effectively with these families is an interdisciplinary process, it would be helpful for judicial officers to meet and confer with counselors and lawyers about making this process as smooth and simple as possible for parents.

The New Ways for Families method described in Chapter 9 is already designed to accomplish the above for those judicial officers and court systems who wish to implement these skills in a coordinated manner. For those who seek training in any of the above methods, please contact www.HighConflictInstitute.com or call 619-221-9108.

CHAPTER TWELVE

Conclusion

TO EVERY EXTENT POSSIBLE, we need to reduce the stress on parents and children in our courts and our society. We need to admit that domestic violence is real, child abuse is real and that child alienation is real, rather than simply fighting about these issues. We need to work together at addressing these issues. We need to admit that our family courts often have a Culture of Blame, which on a prolonged basis can be just as abusive to parents with mental health problems as these parents are to their children.

The court is in a good position to prevent child stress from the start or to reduce it by mandating efforts for positive change by their parents – from ordering parenting programs and classes, to setting limits on emotional attacks during the hearing process. However, if the court does not set standards and impose limits, high-conflict parents will continue to escalate their inappropriate behavior and to impose their inappropriate needs on the children – which leads to alienation and abuse, and possible personality disorders for the next generation.

The judge sets the tone in the case from the very first court hearing – often an emergency hearing in potentially high-conflict cases. Judges who apply the principles described in this book should feel a much better sense of control over their courtrooms and less stress, as their clients are doing more of the work: practicing conflict resolution skills that will help them raise their children out of court, or showing each other's patterns of behavior to more accurately see what needs attention and protective orders.

Any judicial officer can immediately apply many of these concepts to his or her courtroom. I believe that this is important work. You can make a difference on the future of these parents – and especially on the future of their children.

Best wishes!

References

12 A recent study: Epstein, Robert. (2010). What Makes a Good Parent? A scientific analysis ranks the 10 most effective child-rearing practices. Scientific American Mind. November/December 2010, 46.

17-18 Waldie quote: Waldie, Paul. (2008). Judge Wants Divorced Couple to Legally Split–From the Courtroom. The Globe and Mail. May 8, 2008, A12. Used with permission.

21-23 Martinson quote: Martinson, D. J. (2010). One Case-One Specialized Judge: Why Courts Have an Obligation to Manage Alienation and Other High-Conflict Cases. Family Court Review, 48 (1), 180-189. Used with permission.

52-53 Charlenni Ferreira: Graham, T. (2010). Litany of Injuries Opens Child-Abuse Hearing. The Philadelphia Inquirer. January 13, 2010, A1, A4.

56 Child-Inclusive Mediation: McIntosh, J. E., Wells, Y. D., Smyth, B. M., & Long, C. M. (2008). Child-Focused and Child-Inclusive Divorce Mediation: Comparative Outcomes from a Prospective Study of Post separation Adjustment. Family Court Review, 46, 105-124.

57-58 Teicher quote: Teicher, M. H. (2002). Scars That Won't Heal: The Neurobiology of Child Abuse. Scientific American, 286 (3), 68-75, 75. Used with permission.

About the Author

William A. ("Bill") Eddy is a lawyer (Certified Family Law Specialist in California), mediator and therapist (Licensed Clinical Social Worker in California), and the author of several books, including Managing High Conflict People in Court (HCI Press, 2008) and High Conflict People in Legal Disputes (HCI Press, 2006).

He is also the developer of the New Ways for Families method which is being tested in several courts systems in the United States and Canada, as described at www.NewWays4Families.com.

He is the codeveloper of HCI Pattern Analysis, which is described on his website below. His High Conflict Institute provides speakers, training, books and consultations regarding High Conflict People (HCPs) for professionals dealing with legal, workplace, healthcare and educational disputes. Bill's website is www.HighConflictInstitute.com.

WILLIAM A. EDDY, LCSW, JD, CFLS
ATTORNEY and MEDIATOR
President, High Conflict Institute

625 Broadway, Suite 1221   PHONE (619) 221-9108

San Diego, CA 92101   FAX (619) 221-9103

CURRICULUM VITAE

EDUCATION:

University of San Diego School of Law
J.D. received in May 1992
Randolph A. Read Law and Psychiatry Award

San Diego State University
M.S.W., Master of Social Work, May 1981

Case Western Reserve University
B.A., Psychology, May 1970

PROFESSIONAL
LICENSES:

Attorney and Counselor at Law: CA Bar #163236
Licensed by Supreme Court of California
(1992 to present)
Licensed by United States District Court
(1992 to present)
Licensed Clinical Social Worker: CA #LCS12258
(1986 to present)

PROFESSIONAL
CERTIFICATES:

Certified Family Law Specialist, CA Bar
Association (2003 to present)

Practitioner Member, Association of Conflict
Resolution (1994 to 2010)

Credentialed Mediator by National Conflict
Resolution Center (1993 to present)
(Formerly San Diego Mediation Center)

EMPLOYMENT: PRESIDENT, High Conflict Institute
(January 2008 to Present)

Provide training and consultation to judges, attorneys, mediators, human resource professionals,
mental health professionals, healthcare administrators, college administrators and others for disputes involving high conflict personalities. www.
HighConflictInstitute.com.

SENIOR FAMILY MEDIATOR (January 2005 to
Present), National Conflict Resolution Center, San
Diego, CA
Provide divorce mediation services for about 70
couples per year and some business and work-
place mediation.

ADJUNCT FACULTY (2008 to Present)
National Judicial College, Reno, Nevada
Provide occasional training to judges and other
judicial officers at national conferences about managing high-conflict litigants, including family law
judges, Social Security Disability judges, immigra-
tion and national employment (Merit Protection
System Board) judges.

ADJUNCT FACULTY (2009 to Present)
Pepperdine University, School of Law, Malibu, CA
Course in Psychology of Conflict, Straus Dispute
Resolution Center

ATTORNEY and MEDIATOR
Sole Practitioner, San Diego, CA (1993 to 2008)
Family Law and Mediation Practice: Handled
over 400 cases as a family law attorney, over 1000
divorce mediations, and 100 civil mediations.

ADJUNCT PROFESSOR
Negotiation and Mediation Course, 7 Semesters
(1997-2003)
Interviewing and Counseling Difficult Clients
Course (2000)
University of San Diego School of Law

PSYCHOTHERAPIST (CLINICAL SOCIAL WORKER), Counseling & Recovery Institute, San Diego, CA (1987 - 1992)
Psychotherapy for chemically dependent, depressed and divorced adults, their children and families.

PSYCHOTHERAPIST (CLINICAL SOCIAL WORKER)
Mesa Vista Psychiatric Hospital, San Diego, CA (1985 - 1987)
Family therapy and discharge planning for substance abuse and adolescent in-patient units.

TRAININGS
As PRESENTER: 2011

Managing Personality-Disordered Parents – 2-Day Seminar
Association of Family and Conciliation Courts, Baltimore, MD (12/5-6/11)

How to Manage High Conflict People and High Conflict Disputes
Georgia Chapter American Academy of Matrimonial Lawyers (AAML) Atlanta, Georgia (12/2/11)

Working with High Conflict Clients – Ethics and Risk Management
Solutions on Site Seminars, London, Ontario (11/22/11)

Psychology of Conflict Course – Straus Institute of Dispute Resolution
Pepperdine University School of Law, Malibu, CA (11/3-5 & 11/17-19/11)

Understanding and Managing High Conflict People in Legal Disputes
Washington State Bar Association, Seattle, WA (10/24/11)

Advanced Skills for Managing High Conflict Families
Association for Family Law Professionals, Ft. My-

ers, FL (10/21/11)

New Ways for Families – Day Two Training
Medicine Hat Family Services, Medicine Hat,
Alberta (9/30/11)

Working with High Conflict Personalities – Elder
Mediation Training
La Sierra University, Los Angeles, CA (9/21-22/11)

Working with High Conflict Clients – Ethics and
Risk Management
J & K Mental Health Seminars, Lancaster, PA
(9/15/11)

Understanding and Managing High Conflict
People in the Adjudicative Process, Social Security
Administration
Judicial Education Conference, Falls Church, VA
(8/2 and 8/9/11)

Understanding and Managing High Conflict
Clients
Assoc for Conflict Resolution (ACR), Minneapolis,
MN (7/28/11)

New Ways for Families – 2-Day Training
YWCA of Calgary, Calgary, Alberta (6/9-10/11)

Stop Splitting! New Ways for Families with High
Conflict Parents
Assoc of Family and Conciliation Courts, Orlando,
FL (6/2/11)

Mediating with High Conflict People
District Court – Advanced Training, Los Angeles,
CA (5/19/11)

Handling High Conflict Litigants
Maryland Court of Appeals Judicial Conference,
Annapolis, MD (5/13/11)

Understanding and Managing High Conflict Personalities
Mediation and Restorative Justice Center, Edmon-
ton, Alberta (4/27-28/11)

Managing High Conflict Personalities in Health
Care
ABA Dispute Resolution Section Conference, Den-
ver, CO (4/15/11)

Managing High Conflict Personalities in Family
Law Cases
Familjerättssocionomernas Riksförening, Malmo,
Sweden (3/17/11)

Family Law – Handling High Conflict Personali-
ties
British Columbia Continuing Legal Education,
Vancouver, BC (3/9/11)

Managing High Conflict Personalities in Health
Care
ABA Health Law Section Conference, New Or-
leans, LA (2/23/11)

New Ways for Families – A New Interdisciplinary
Method for Managing Potentially High Conflict
Families

Assoc of Family and Conciliation Courts, San
Francisco, CA (2/13/11)

Working with High Conflict Personalities
Erickson Mediation Institute, Minneapolis, MN
(2/4/11)

Understanding and Managing High Conflict
People
Intel Human Resource Professionals, Chandler, AZ
(1/12/11)

2010

High Conflict People in Mediation
Georgia Office of Dispute Resolution, Atlanta, GA
(12/10/10)

Understanding and Managing High Conflict
People
Municipal Code Enforcement Officers, Missis-
sauga, Ontario (11/15-17/10)

Psychology of Conflict Course – Straus Institute of
Dispute Resolution
Pepperdine University School of Law, Malibu, CA
(11/4-6 & 11/18-20/10)

Managing High Conflict Situations on Campus
Mt. Royal University, Calgary, Alberta, Canada
(11/8/10 and 11/9/10)

Dealing with High Conflict People - Treating Difficult D.V. Men Program
Relationship Training Institute, San Diego, CA
(11/6/10)

New Ways for Families – A New Team Method for
High Conflict Parents
International Academy of Collaborative Profes-
sionals, Wash, DC (10/30/10)

Understanding High Conflict Persons in Family
Law Cases
Iowa State Bar Association CLE, Des Moine, Iowa
(10/28/10)

Personality Disorders and Family Violence
San Diego Protective Services, San Diego, CA
(10/11/10)

It's All Your Fault! Managing High Conflict People
in Legal Disputes
San Diego District Attorney – All Hands Day, San
Diego, CA (10/11/10)

Understanding and Managing High Conflict
People
National Judicial College program for Immigra-
tion Courts
Reno, Nevada (10/8/10)

Understanding and Managing High Conflict People
in the Adjudicative Process, Social Security Administration Falls Church, Virginia (8/3/10 and 8/10/10)

New Ways for Families – Four Advanced Skills
Mediate West, Mission Viejo, CA (8/5/10)

Ethically Handling the High Conflict Client
Family Law Paralegal Program, San Diego, CA
(7/28/10)

New Ways for Families
San Diego County Bar Association, San Diego, CA
(6/27/10)

New Ways for Families – Basic Training for Family
Law Professionals, High Conflict Institute, Seattle,
WA (6/23/10)

Managing High Conflict People in Legal Disputes
High Conflict Institute, Seattle, WA (6/22/10)

Managing High Conflict People in Mediation
Bellevue Neighborhood Association, Bellevue, WA
(6/21/10)

Managing High Conflict People in Family Law
Disputes and New Ways for Families Overview
Maryland Collaborative Practice Council, Colum-
bia, MD (6/4/10)

New Ways for Families Training
Association of Family and Conciliation Courts
Annual Conference, Denver, Colorado (6/2/10)

Dealing with Difficult People in the Courtroom
National Judicial College Training, Sanibel Island,
Florida (5/25/10)

Working with Cluster B Personality Disorders
California Association of Marriage and Family
Therapists, Carlsbad, California (5/21/10)

Understanding and Managing High Conflict Personalities
Oregon Mediation Association, Portland, Oregon
(5/14/10)

Dealing with Difficult Personalities

Community Mediation Services, Eugene, Oregon (5/13/10)

Understanding and Managing High Conflict Disputes
American Association of Matrimonial Lawyers (AAML) and
American Institute for Certified Public Accountants (AICPA)
Annual Conference on Divorce, Las Vegas, NV (5/7/10)

Managing High Conflict Personalities and New Ways for Families
Harford County Circuit Court, Harford, Maryland (5/4/10)

Managing High Conflict People in Legal Disputes and New Ways for Families Basic and Advanced Trainings
High Conflict Forum, Toronto, Ontario, Canada (4/28-29/10)

Managing High-Conflict Parents
National Council of Juvenile and Family Court Judges
Annual National Conference, Las Vegas, NV (3/16/10)

Understanding and Managing High Conflict People in Legal Disputes
Washington State Bar Association, Seattle, WA (2/19/10)

Managing High-Conflict Clients in Divorce
Advanced Symposium, Institute for Divorce Financial Analysts
Las Vegas, NV (2/11/10)

Law and Ethics Update 2010, Biannual Training Update
Kaiser Permanente, Department of Psychiatry, San Diego, CA (1/19/10)

2009

Understanding and Managing High Conflict Personalities
Association of Psychologists of Nova Scotia, Halifax, Canada (10/24/09)

Managing High Conflict People in Legal Disputes and New Ways for Families Basic and Advanced Trainings
Medicine Hat, Alberta, Canada (10/2-3/09)

New Ways for Families Basic and Advanced Trainings
Victoria Collaborative Law Group, Victoria, BC (9/30/09)

Understanding and Managing High Conflict Personalities
Washington State Bar Association, Elder Law Conference, Seattle, WA(9/18/09)

Understanding and Managing High Conflict Personalities
Cook County Judicial Training, Chicago, IL (9/17/09)

Handling High Conflict Clients – Family Law Section Webinar
Canadian Bar Association – Alberta, Canada (9/15/09)

Working with High Conflict People, Inns of Court Program, Vista, CA (9/15/09)

Understanding and Managing Difficult People in Court
National Judicial College Training, Phoenix, AZ (9/14/09)

Bullies in the Workplace, Association for Conflict Resolution, Workplace Section Teleseminar (8/26/09)

Five Personality Disorders in High Conflict Mediation
Family Mediation Canada, Webinar, Canada
(8/5/09)

Managing High Conflict People in Legal Disputes and New Ways for Families Basic and Advanced Trainings, High Conflict Institute, Seattle, WA
(7/23-24/09)

Understanding and Managing High Conflict People in Court
Social Security Administration Judicial Conference, San Francisco, CA (7/15/09

Understanding and Managing High Conflict People in Court
2009 Arizona Judicial Conference, Scottsdale, AZ
(6/19/09)

Understanding and Managing High Conflict Personalities
Victoria Collaborative Law Group, Victoria, BC
(6/15/09)

Understanding and Managing High Conflict Personalities
British Columbia Mediation Roster Society, Vancouver, BC (6/13/09)

Working with High Conflict Clients
Santa Barbara Inns of Court, Santa Barbara, CA
(6/3/09)

New Ways for Families, Association of Family and Conciliation Courts
Annual International Conference, New Orleans, LA (5/28/09)

Understanding and Managing High Conflict People
Mental Health Association of Southwest Florida, Naples, FL (5/15/09)

Dealing with Difficult People During Divorce,

Collaborative Family Law Group of Southern Arizona, Tucson, AZ (5/9/09)

Handling High Conflict People
Judicial Seminar on Self-Represented Litigants, Washington DC Superior Court Judges, Washington, DC (5/7/09)

Innovations in Family Law, Panel Speaker, Combined ADR and Family Law Sections, San Diego County Bar Association, San Diego, CA (5/4/09)

New Ways for Families, Short Presentation to San Diego Family Court Judges Retreat, San Diego, CA (5/1/09)

Handling High Conflict People
U. S. Merit Systems Protection Board, Annual Conference, Indianapolis, IN (4/29/09)

Understanding and Managing High Conflict Personalities
Professional Standards Conference, Calgary Police Service, Calgary, Canada (4/27/09)

Understanding and Managing High Conflict Personalities in Legal Disputes
Louisiana State Bar Association, Family Law Section, New Orleans, LA (4/24/09)

Mediation with High Conflict Personalities
Tennessee Association of Professional Mediators, Nashville, TN (3/27/09)

New Ways for Families, Training for Family Law Attorneys, Counselors and Judges, University of San Diego, San Diego, CA (3/13/09)

Understanding and Managing High Conflict Personalities in Legal Disputes, University of San Diego, San Diego, CA (3/12/09)

2002-2008

Trainings provided prior to 2009 available on request

TRAININGS
ATTENDED: Numerous International, National, State and Local
                Conferences and Seminars on Dispute Resolution,
                Family Law, Clinical Social Work and Mediation
                (1980 - Present)

PROFESSIONAL
ASSOCIATIONS: CALIFORNIA STATE BAR ASSOCIATION
                ACADEMY OF PROFESSIONAL FAMILY
                MEDIATORS
                ASSOCIATION OF FAMILY AND
                CONCILIATION COURTS
                ASSOCIATION FOR CONFLICT RESOLUTION
                INTERNATIONAL ACADEMY OF
                COLLABORATIVE PROFESSIONALS
                INTERNATIONAL ACADEMY OF LAW AND
                MENTAL HEALTH
                NATIONAL ASSOCIATION OF SOCIAL
                WORKERS
                NATIONAL ORGANIZATION OF FORENSIC
                SOCIAL WORKERS
                SOCIETY FOR CLINICAL SOCIAL WORK
                SAN DIEGO COLLABORATIVE FAMILY LAW
                GROUP SAN DIEGO COUNTY BAR
                ASSOCIATION
                SOUTHERN CALIFORNIA MEDIATION
                ASSOCIATION

PUBLICATIONS: SPLITTING: Protecting Yourself While Divorcing
                Someone with Borderline or Narcissistic
                Personality Disorder, A book for clients in difficult
                divorces, and their therapists and attorneys. New
                Harbinger Press, Oakland, CA (2011)

                BIFF: Quick Responses to High Conflict People
                (For anyone) HCI Press, Scottsdale, AZ (2011)

                New Ways for Families:
                Professional Guidebook (2009)
                Parent Workbook (2009)
                Collaborative Parent Workbook (2009)

                "It's All YOUR Fault!" 12 Tips for Managing

People Who Blame Others For Everything, HCI Press, Scottsdale, AZ (2008)

MANAGING HIGH CONFLICT PEOPLE IN COURT (Specifically for Judges), HCI Press, Scottsdale, AZ (2008)

HIGH CONFLICT PEOPLE IN LEGAL DISPUTES HCI Press, Scottsdale, AZ (2006, 2008)

THE SPLITTING CD: An Interview with William Eddy, Author of SPLITTING, Eggshells Press, Milwaukee, Wisconsin (2006)

Handling High Conflict Personalities in Family Mediation, ACResolution Quarterly Magazine of the Association for Conflict Resolution Summer 2005, Washington, DC.

HIGH CONFLICT PERSONALITIES. Self-published (2003). Re-issued as High Conflict People in Legal Disputes by HCI Press (2008)

How Personality Disorders Drive Family Court Litigation, VOIR DIRE, Magazine of the Solano County Bar Association, March/April 2000.

Dealing with Difficult Clients, CALIFORNIA LAWYER, Jan. 1999, p. 33.

YOUR COUNSELOR AT LAW Newsletter (1997 - 2005) Negotiating Your Divorce, 70-Page Booklet, Self-Published 1997

Mediating Economic Issues in Divorce: An Ethical Debate in Three Acts, 31 FAMILY AND CONCILI-ATION COURTS REVIEW 354 (July, 1993)

Working With Addicted Parents, THE CONNEC-TION: Newsletter for National CASA Association, Advocates for Abused Children (1993)

Motivating Substance Abusing Parents in Dependency Court, 43 JUVENILE & FAMILY COURT JOURNAL 11 (1992)

ON-TARGET PARENTING: A SELF-TRAINING MANUAL FOR RECOVERING PARENTS, Lead author, Self-published (1991, 2000)

Couples in Recovery: Four-Stage Approach for Intimacy Restoration, FOCUS: EDUCATING PROFESSIONALS IN FAMILY RECOVERY (July 1989)

INTERNET TRAININGS PROVIDED:	"Its All Your Fault" – Working with High Conflict Personalities (July 2004 to Present) www.ContinuingEdCourses.net, 8-Hours of CEUs for Psychologists, Clinical Social Workers and other Mental Health Professionals
WEBSITES:	www.HighConflictInstitute.com and www.NewWays4Families.com

More Books from HCI Press at www.hcipress.com

CPSIA information can be obtained
at www.ICGtesting.com
Printed in the USA
JSHW032134161222
35059JS00005B/9